INDIAN EMINENT RESEARCHERS AND THEIR CONTRIBUTION

DR. GANESH R. SANAP | DR. SHOEB R. SAYYED

Contents

Preface

Some great Indian scientists and researchers have made noteworthy contributions to the world and have garnered a praising synonym in the science field of India. India has been scientifically advanced from ancient times to the contemporary world. India is a land of creativity and originality. Sovereignty has given great minds to explore ideas that have made it to global recognition. some Famous Indian Scientists who made noteworthy contributions in the world have made us proud time after time. The world has always been complex, but the inventions of these great Indian scientists in the field of science have given solutions to the problems raised.

As a country, we should feel immensely proud of their mammoth contributions, but as an individual, our lives have become secure and easy due to their scientific inventions. Indian scientists and researchers have contributed to the development of the specific subject field. Some of the prominent researcher have created or formed the new stream. Most of the Indian scientist and researchers have given solutions, innovations, thoughts, etc. not only for the India but for the world also.

The present book attempts to review some great Indian scientists and researchers contributions in the various subject discipline. The purpose of this book is to introduce the work or the contribution of these great personalities in the development of society in the form of their inventions or the theory.

-Editors

CHAPTER ONE

The Father of Indian Library Science: Dr. S. R. Ranganathan

-Dr. Ganesh Ramdas Sanap

1. Introduction:

The man who have developed library science in india, the man whose contributions to library and information science have had a global impact., the name of the the most prominent personality is Padma Shree Dr. Shiyali Ramamrita Ranganathan. Dr. Eugene Garfield have mentioned in his article entitled 'Tribute to S.R. Ranganathan' that "Dr. Ranganathan is to library science what Einstein is to physics" Dr. S. R. Ranganathan is known as the father of library science. Although it was not his original career, he devoted his life to the library profession. He was a teacher, a researcher, a writer, and an advocate. He founded and served on numerous committees and organizations, including establishing the Documentation Research Training Centre. Throughout his career Ranganathan advocated for school libraries and had a strong belief in the importance of libraries in schools for the creation of an educated society.

Dr. S. R. Ranganathan made innumerable contributions to library science, but is most remembered for two: The Five Laws of Library Science and his Colon Classification System (CCS). The Five Laws have served as an anchor and a guiding light to the library profession for decades. They clearly and concisely distill the essence of the library mission, and remain relevant even 87 years after their original publication. The Colon

Classification System is a cataloguing structure devised by Dr.S. R. Ranganathan. The name is derived from the fact that the call numbers created using this scheme are broken up by punctuation, including colons. While the Colon Classification System may not be widely used, understanding the basic theory behind it is a valuable tool for librarians.

1. The Life of Dr. S. R. Ranganathan:

Shiyali Ramamrita Ranganathan was born on 9th August 1892 to Mr. Ramamrita Iyer and Mrs. Sitalakshmi at Ubhayavedantapuram, a small hamlet in the Tanjore District of Madras Presidency (present day Tamil Nadu). Ranganathan lost his father in 1898 when he was only 6 years old. He had his school education in the town of Shiyali (Shirgazhi), his mother's native town, and continued there till he completed his matriculation in 1909. Ranganathan spent his childhood and school days as member of an orthodox South Indian Brahmin family. Even when he was still studying, at the age of 15, he was married to Rukmani. Ranganathan moved to Madras (now, Chennai) for higher education. Ranganathan attended the S.M. Hindu High School at Shiyali and passed Matriculation examination in 1908-1909. Ranganathan passed the examination in First Class, in spite of sickness like anaemia, piles, and stammering. In his high school career, he came under the influence of P.A. Subramanya Ayyar, a scholar on Sri Aurobindo. Ranganathan joined the junior intermediate class at the Madras Christian College in March 1909. Even in those days, there were paucity of college seats. Ranganathan was picked up for his excellent marks in all the subjects and the principal. Prof. Skinner spotted him in a crowd of students and admitted him into the course. Ranganathan passed B.A. with a first class in March/April 1913. In June, same year, he joined for the M.A. course in Mathematics with Professor Edward B. Ross as his teacher. Being a favourite student of Prof. Ross, Ranganathan had an excellent Guru-Shishya relationship.

Ranganathan began his professional life as a mathematician, and he was successively a member of the mathematics faculties at universities in Mangalore, Coimbatore and Madras. As a mathematics professor, he published a handful of papers, mostly on the history of mathematics. His career as an educator was somewhat hindered by a handicap of stammering.

In 1923, the University of Madras created the post of University Librarian to oversee their poorly organized collection. Among the 900 applicants for the position, none had any formal training in librarianship, and Ranganathan's' handful of papers satisfied the search committee's requirement that the candidate should have a research background. His sole knowledge of librarianship came from an Encyclopædia Britannica article he read days before the interview.

Ranganathan was initially reluctant to pursue the position (he had forgotten about his application by the time he was called for an interview there). To his own surprise, he received the appointment and accepted the position in January 1924.Ranganathan found the solitude of the position was intolerable. After a matter of weeks, complaining of total boredom, he went back to the university administration to beg for his teaching position back. A deal was struck that Ranganthan would travel to London to study contemporary Western practices in librarianship, and that, if he returned and still rejected librarianship as a career, the mathematics lectureship would be his again.

Ranganathan travelled to University College London, which at that time housed the only graduate degree program in library science in Britain. At University College, he earned marks only slightly above average, but his mathematical mind latched onto the problem of classification, a subject typically taught by rote in library programs of the time. As an outsider, he focused on what he perceived to be flaws with the popular decimal classification, and began to explore new possibilities on his own.

He began drafting the system that was ultimately to become the Colon Classification while in England, and refined it as he returned home, even going so far as to reorder the ship's library on the voyage back to India. He initially got the idea for the system from seeing a set of Meccano in a toy store in London. Ranganathan returned with great interest for libraries and librarianship and a vision of its importance for the Indian nation. He returned to and held the position of University Librarian at the University of Madras for twenty years. During that time, he helped to found the Madras Library Association in 1928, and lobbied actively for the establishment of free public libraries throughout India and for the creation of a comprehensive national library.

Ranganathan was considered by many to be a workaholic. During his two decades in Madras, he consistently worked 13-hour days, seven days a week, without taking a vacation for the entire time. The first few years of Ranganathan's tenure at Madras were years of deliberation and analysis as he addressed the problems of library administration and classification. It was during this period that he produced what have come to be known as his two greatest legacies: his five laws of library science (1931) and the colon classification system (1933).

After two decades of serving as librarian at Madras, a post he had intended to keep until his retirement, Ranganathan retired from his position after conflicts with a new university vice-chancellor became intolerable. At the age of 54, he submitted his resignation and, after a brief bout with depression, accepted a professorship in library science at Banaras Hindu University in Varanasi, his last formal academic position, in August 1945. There, he catalogued the university's collection; by the time he left four years later, he had classified over 100,000 items personally.

In spite of the good salary he earned, he adopted a Gandhi-like simplicity in diet and dress. He ate only lightly, shunned coffee and tea, and wore plain homespun garments. He usually walked barefoot to the library and worked there barefoot, saying that the library was his home, and no one wears shoes in his own home. As for his real home, it was sparsely furnished and lacked electricity, although he could have easily afforded these amenities. The money he saved through years of frugal living, he gave away twice. In 1925 to endow a mathematics fellowship at Madras Christian College in honour of his mathematics professor, Edward B.Ross, and In 1956 to endow the Sarada Ranganathan chair of library science at the University of Madras.

Ranganathan headed the Indian Library Association from 1944 to 1953, but was never a particularly adept administrator, and left amid controversy when the Delhi Public Library chose to use the Dewey Decimal Classification system instead of his own Colon Classification. He held an honorary professorship at Delhi University from 1949 to 1955 and helped build that institution's library science programs with S. Dasgupta, a former student of his. In 1951, Ranganathan released an album on Folkways Records entitled, Readings from the Ramayana: In Sanskrit Bhagavad Gita.

Ranganathan's final major achievement was the establishment of the Documentation Research and Training Centre as a department and research centre in the Indian Statistical Institute in Bangalore in 1962, where he served as honorary director for five years. In 1965, the Indian government honoured him for his contributions to the field with a rare title of "National Research Professor." In the final years of his life, Ranganathan finally succumbed to ill health, and was largely confined to his bed. On September 27, 1972, he died of complications from bronchitis. Dr. S R Ranganathan is considered to be the father, the doyen, messiah of library and information profession in India.

3. **Contribution of Dr. S. R. Ranganathan:**

• **Colon Classification**

Ranganathan's chief technical contributions to library science were in classification and indexing theory. His Colon Classification (1933) introduced a system that is widely used in research libraries around the world and that has affected the evolution of such older systems as the Dewey Decimal Classification. Later he devised the technique of chain indexing for deriving subject-index entries. Colon Classification is the system of library organization developed by Ranganathan in 1933. It is general rather than specific in nature, and it can create complex or new categories through the use of facets, or colons. In it, there are 108 main classes and 10 generalized classes (broadly divided between the humanities and sciences), which are represented by a mixed notation of Arabic numerals and Roman and Greek letters. Each main class comprises five fundamental facets, or groups: personality, matter, energy, Space, time. Ranganathan's main contribution to classification was the notion of these fundamental facets, or categories. Instead of schedules of numbers for each topic, Colon Classification uses series of short tables from which component numbers are chosen and linked by colons to form a whole. The book number is an integral part of the call number, a departure from Dewey or Library of Congress systems. Each main class has its appropriate facets and focuses; e.g., literature has language and form. In addition, there are four floating tables that correspond to subdivisions -- e.g., form, geography, time, and language. Further expansion of the tables is allowed through colon addition or omission (if the subject cannot be expanded). The collection of the University of Madras, India, was utilized in the creation of Colon Classification.

• **The Five Laws of Library Science:**

The 5 Laws of Library Science is a theory proposed by S. R. Ranganathan in 1931, detailing the principles of operating a library system. Five laws of library science are called the set of norms, percepts, and guides to good practice in librarianship. Many librarians worldwide accept them as the foundations of their philosophy. Dr. S.R. Ranganathan conceived the Five Laws of Library Science in 1924. The statements embodying these laws were formulated in 1928. These laws were first published in Ranganathan's classic book entitled Five Laws of Library Science in 1931. (Haider, 2023)

These laws are:

i. Books are for use
ii. Every reader his/her book
iii. Every book its reader
iv. Save the time of the reader
v. The library is a growing organism

- **Classified Catalogue Code**

Classified Catalogue Code is another important work by Dr. S R Ranganathan. It is published in the year 1934. In this book he maintained that, a catalogue should consist of two components. One part should be classified by subject, reflecting the library's classification system, with class number entries. The other should be a dictionary catalogue, including author, title, series, and similar identifiers, as well as alphabetized subject entries. The function of a catalogue is to intimate works so they can be found by author, title, series, and so forth. It must also allow readers to review the selection of works on a given subject

- **Chain Index:**

To determine subject entries for the dictionary catalogue, Ranganathan developed a simple method called chain indexing. This method simply uses each facet of a subject, together with its immediately preceding facets, as an index entry. Thus, all important aspects of the subject, from the most general to the most specific, are automatically covered. Chain indexing can be adapted to other classification systems as well.

- **Establishment of the Documentation Research and Training Centre:**

In 1962, Ranganathan founded the Documentation Research & Training Centre (DRTC) as a unit of the Indian Statistical Institute, where he served as honorary director for five years. The academic programme of DRTC was specially designed to train information specialists capable of designing and running information support systems for R&D and industry. In 1965, the Indian government honoured him for his contributions to the field with a rare title of "National Research Professor."

- **Library Movement:**

During the working as an academic librarian in Madras University, he also realized the role of the public library in the country and the social and cultural development of the country. So, he initiated a library Association for the enforcement of public library Act in the Madras Presidency with the support of local political leaders and other eminent people in the Madras . This step causes the establishment of Madras Library Association (MALA) in 1928. He also drafted library legislation act for the states.After several efforts and labor by Ranganathan causes first library act in Madras at 1948 by his first effort and milestone presently 19 states have its own library legislation in India.

Ranganathan also served as president of the Indian Library Association from 1944 to 1953. He also founded the Mysore Library Association (now Karnataka State Library Association) and the Indian Association of Teachers of Library Science (IATLIS) (now, Indian Association of Teachers of Library and Information Science).

Ranganathan was one of the founders of the Indian National Scientific Documentation Centre (INSDOC) established in 1952 under the Council of Scientific and Industrial Research (CSIR) with support from UNESCO to provide information support services for R&D activities. He was also chair of its first Scientific Advisory Committee. INSDOC was merged with NISCOM (National Institute of Science Communication), also a unit of CSIR, in 2002 to form NISCAIR (National Institute of Science Communication and Information Resources).

4. **Honours and awards:**

Ranganathan was recipient of many honours and awards. Some noteworthy awards are:

- Rao Saheb (in 1935 from the Government of India under British rule)
- doctorate honoris causa (University of Delhi, 1948)

- honorary fellow, Virginia Bibliographic Society, 1951
- honorary member, Indian Association of Special Libraries and Information Centres, 1956
- padmashri (from the Government of India in 1957)
- honorary vice-president, Library Association (London), 1957
- honorary fellow, International Federation for Documentation, 1957
- honorary DLitt (University of Pittsburg, 1964)
- honorary fellow, Indian Standards Institution, 1967
- national research professor (Government of India, 1965)
- Margaret Mann citation (American Library Association, 1970; the very first time the citation was presented to a person from outside USA)
- grand knight of peace, Mark Twain Society, U.S.A., 1971

5. **Books written by Dr. S. R. Ranganathan:**

- The Five Laws of Library Science, 1931
- Colon Classification, 1933
- Classified Cataloguing Code, 1934
- Prolegomena to Library Classification, 1937
- Prolegomena to Library Classification (2nd ed.), 1957
- Prolegomena to Library Classification (3rd Ed.), 1967
- Classification and Communication, 1951
- Documentation: Genesis and Development, 1973
- Documentation and its facets, 1963
- Reference Service, 1961
- Library Book Selection, 1952
- Library Book Selection (2nd ed.), 1966
- Philosophy of Library Classification, 1951
- Library Administration, 1935
- Library Manual, 1951
- Ramanujan: The man and the mathematician, 1967
- Suggestion for the organization of the Libraries in India, 1946
- Heading and Canons, 1955
- A Librarian Looks Back: An autobiography of Dr. S. R. Rangnathan (Editor: P. N. Kaula), 1992
- Colon Classification (1 " ed.), 1933
- Colon Classification (2nd ed.), 1939
- Colon Classification (3rd ed.), 1950

- Colon Classification (4h ed.), 1952
- Colon Classification (5th ed.), 1957
- Colon Classification (6th ed.), 1960

Conclusion:

Libraries play a vital role in the development of a country. Dr S. R. Ranganathan, who is known as "Father of Library Science in India", was the first person who identified the real need of libraries and library science education in our country. Dr S. R. Ranganathan is known as the father of library science for a reason. The profession as a whole owes him a debt of gratitude not only for his material contributions, but for his dedication to his work. He devoted his life to the improvement and advancement of libraries and the library profession. The Five Laws of Library Science continue to be relevant to librarians in all settings. The Laws inspire and motivate. The CCS may not be widely used, but it demonstrates the value of multidimensional understanding of library materials, particularly with regard to cataloguing and retrieving information.

References:

Garfield, Eugene (1984). Tribute to S.R. Ranganathan (Current Contents N 7, 13 February,)

Ranganathan S. R. (1963). *The five laws of library science* ([Ed. 2 reprinted with minor amendments]). Asia Pub. House.

Allen, K. (1978). *Encyclopedia of Library and Information Science.* New York: Marcel Dekker Inc.

Babu, B.R. (2011). Relevance of Five Laws of Library Science in the Contemporary Library World. *Journal of The Korean Society for Library and Information Science, 45,* 253-269.

S. R. Ranganathan. (2023, February 2). Retrieved from Librarianship Studies & Information Technology: https://www.librarianshipstudies.com/2019/02/s-r-ranganathan.html

Haider, S. (2023, Feb. 2). *Five Laws of Library Science.* Retrieved from Librarianship Studies & Information Technology: https://www.librarianshipstudies.com/2017/09/five-laws-of-library-science.html

Bhatt, R. K. (2011). "Relevance of Ranganathan's Laws of Library Science in Library Marketing" *Library Philosophy and Practice (e-journal).* 551.

CHAPTER TWO

The Most Famous Chemist from India

-Dr. Pravin N. Chavan

Chemistry is a living subject that covers every element of the environment. Every element of the environment is made up of chemistry, selection chemistry is considered an important subject. Medicines Fertilizers Metals etc. to increase the importance of this subject. They have a big share. Any drug, fertilizer, metals and other products are made from this chemical.

In today's era, the competition is going on in every country in the country to make new and sophisticated weapons. Chemicals are used to make weapons, at the same time medicines, fertilizers, metals etc. are made from chemicals. Hence, Chemistry subject is respected and looked upon in the world. In every country of the world there is a competition to master this subject

If we look at the Nobel Prizes so far, most of the Nobel Prizes have been won in chemistry. The Nobel Prize is considered the world's highest research honor. This subject is as vast as the ocean. Indian scientists have also made a great contribution in the subject as follows:

- **Venkatraman Ramakrishnan :**

Venkataraman Ramakrishnan was born on April 1, 1952 in Cuddalore, Tamil Nadu. His father was a physicist named CV Raman and mother's name was Rajalakshmi Ramakrishan. Raman Radhakrishnan's research subject is Biochemistry and Biophysics (Common root: Tamil Nadu gets its third laureate, 8 oct 2009). Research topics of Venkataraman- Structure and function of the ribosome, macromolecular, crystallography. Venkataraman

Ramakrishnan received the following Awards- Knight Bachelor in 2012(No. 60009, 31 Dec 2011), Padma Vibhushan in 2010, Nobel Prize in Chemistry 2009, Louis-Jeantet Prize for Medicine in 2007, Member of the National Academy of Sciences in 2004. Venkatraman Ramakrishnan is an Indian-born British and American structural biologist who shared the 2009 Nobel Prize in Chemistry with T. A. Steitz and A. Yonath, "for studies of the structure and function of the ribosome" (2009 Chemistry Nobel Laureates, 14 Oct 2009). Since 1999, he has worked as a group leader at the Medical Research Council Laboratory of Molecular Biology on the Cambridge Biomedical Campus, UK and is a Fellow of Trinity College, Cambridge, England. He served as President of the Royal Society from 2015 to 2020 (Fernández, et al., 15 Nov 2013), **(Amunts, et al., 28 March 2014)**.

- **Kamala Sohonie :**

Kamala Sohonie is the second most famous Indian chemist. She was born in 8 June 1912 in Indore. Her Ph.D. awarded on scientific discipline topic(Arvind, 19 Oct 2019), **(Tha Glass Ceiling:The why and therefore , 6 March 2012)**.

This work was conducted in the Indian Institute of Science, Bangalore, paved the way for women to be accepted into the institution for the first time in it is history (How Kamala Sohonie Defied Gender Bias & Became the First Indian Woman PhD in Science, 20 Jan 2017). Her research delved into the effects of various vitamins and into the nutritive values of pulses, paddy, and groups of food items consumed by some of the poorest sections of the Indian population. Her work on the nutritional benefits of the palm extract called 'Neera' was inspired by the then-president Rajendra Prasad's suggestion. Kamala Sohonie received the Rashtrapati Award for this work (Ritesh, 7 March 2017).

- **Asima Chatterjee :**

She is the third most famous Indian chemist. He born in 23 September, 1917 (Google honours Indian chemist Asima Chatterjee on 100th birthday, 23 Feb 2017). Her research work topics on vinca alkaloids, the development of anti-epileptic drugs, and development of anti-malarial drugs. She has work on medicinal plants of the Indian subcontinent. She was the first woman to receive a Doctorate of Science from an Indian university. Asima

Chatterjee was awarded Ph.D. in 1944 by the University of Calcutta (Chatterjee, 6 Dec 2019).

She was first women to award the Ph.D. by an Indian university. She was elected as the General President of the Indian Science Congress, a premier institution that oversees scientific research. The S. S. Bhatnagar award, the C V Raman award, and the P C Ray award; and is the recipient of the Padma Bhushan in 1960. She has work on natural products with special reference to medicinal chemistry(The Shaping of Indian Science. , 2003).

She was published more than four hundred research articles in national and international journals, it includes reviews. She also was published books with citations. Her work as a professor in Brabourne College, U.S.A.
After her return to India in 1950, she has been starting research work on alkaloids and coumarins with renewed vigour **(Pakrashi, 2012)**.

Her work on Rauwolfia species brought her into close association with the late Professor Dr. Salimuzzaman Siddiqui, FRS, former Director of Hussein Ebrahim Jamal Post Graduate Institute of Chemistry, University of Karachi, Pakistan(Women Scientists of India: Dr. Asima Chatterjee – Google Arts & Culture, 23 Sep 2017).

- **Chintamani Nagesa Ramachandra Rao (C.N.R. Rao) :**

CNR Rao was born in 30 June 1934 in Mysore, Karnataka. He has graduate from Mysore University, post graduate from Banaras Hindu University & Ph.D. degree awarded in Purdue University. He was youngest lecturer in Indian institute of science (1959). He has been published more than 1774 research articles with citations. He also published 54 books(2011), 22 Feb 2014).

He has won various awards such as Marlour medal in 1967, shanti Swarup Bhatnagar Prize for Science & Technologies in 1969, Hughus Medal in 2000, Indian Science award in 2004, Dan David Prize in 2005, Legion of Honor in 2005, Abdus Salam Medal in 2008, Royal Medal in 2009, Padma Shri in 1974, Padma Vibhushan in 1985, Karnataka Ratna in 2001, Bharat Ratna in 2014, order of Friendship 2009, National Order of Scientific merit in 2012, Order of Rising Sun in 2015. He was chairperson of Scientific Advisory council to the prime Minister of India from 1985 to 1989 and 2005 to 2014. He also works in Jawaharlal Nehru Centre for advanced Scientific Research & International centre for material science (C. N.R Rao and his contributions, 11 March 2011).

His research work on Solid State & Structural Chemistry. His work on transition metal oxide has led to basic understanding of novel phenomena and the relationship between materials properties and the structural chemistry of these materials. Rao was one of the earliest to synthesise two-dimensional oxide materials such as La2CuO4. He was one of the first to synthesis 123-cuprates, the first liquid nitrogen-temperature superconductor in 1987. He was also the first to synthesis Y- junction carbon nanotubes in the mid-1990s. His work has led to a systematic study of compositionally controlled metal-insulator transitions. Such studies have had a profound impact in application fields such as colossal magneto resistance and high temperature superconductivity. Oxide semiconductors have unusual promise. He has made immense contributions to nanomaterials over the last two decades, besides his work on hybrid materials (Rao, 10 Sep 2016).

- **Yellapragada Subba Rao :**

Yellapragada Subba Rao was born in Bhimavaram Madras at 12 January 1895. He was an Indian biochemist who discovered the function of adenosine triphosphate as an energy source in the cell (Koscak, 1 March 2019).

He developed methotrexate for the treatment of cancer and led the department at Lederle Laboratories. Benjamin Minge Duggar discovered chlortetracycline (auromycin) in 1945. A student of Madras Medical College, his elder brother and younger brother both died of tropical sprue within a period of eight days(Kapur, 1998).

He has since discovered folic acid as a treatment for tropical sprue. He also discovered methotrexate, a chemotherapy drug he invented that is still used today and is also used for rheumatoid arthritis, and diethylcarbamazine remains the only effective drug for the treatment of filariasis. He is credited with the first synthesis of the chemical compound's folic acid and methotrexate. Subbarao died of a heart attack in America (Gupta, 2002).

- **Darshan Ranganathan :**

Darshan Ranganathan was born on 4 June, 1941 in Delhi. She was Graduated, post-graduated and doctoral degree in chemistry from Delhi

University. She was lecturer in chemistry at Miranda College, Delhi.

Ranganathan's special passion was reproducing natural biochemical processes in the laboratory. She created a protocol which achieved the autonomous reproduction of imidazole, an ingredient of histidine and histamine with pharmaceutical importance. She also developed a working simulation of the urea cycle. As her career developed, she became a specialist in designing proteins to hold a wide variety of different conformations and designing nanostructures using self-assembling peptides (Dasgupta, 6 June 2022).

She has research in organic chemistry subject. Fellow of the Indian Academy of Science; TWAS Prize in Chemistry in 1999, Senior Research Scholarship of the Royal Commission for the Exhibition of 1851. A.V. Rama Rao Foundation Award, Jawaharlal Nehru Birth Centenary Visiting Fellowship, and Sukh Dev Endowment Lectureship (Khan, 19 March 2019).

- **Gautam Radhakrishnan Desiraju :**

Gautam Desiraju was born 21 August, 1952 in Madras India. Research fields of Gautam Radhakrishna Desiraju are crystal engineering and weak hydrogen bonding(G.R., Crystal Engineering. The Design of Organic Solids, 1989).

He has published books on these subjects in 1989 and 1999. He has co-authored a textbook in crystal engineering in 2011 (Desiraju, 2011).

Gautam Desiraju contribution to the subject of crystal engineering has focus on the concept of the supramolecular synthon, which is a small sub-structural unit that is an adequate enough representation of the entire crystal structure of a molecular solid. The major problem in crystal engineering is that the prediction of a crystal structure from a molecular structure is very difficult and not easily derivable from functional groups. Identification of supramolecular synthons simplifies this otherwise intractable problem(G.R., Supramolecular Synthons in Crystal Engineering. A New Organic Synthesis, 1995).

The supramolecular synthon concept is now widely used by crystal engineers in the design of molecular crystals and pharmaceutical co-crystals, which are important from scientific and commercial viewpoints. Crystal engineering is effectively like supramolecular synthesis in the solid state, and there is a direct analogy between the supramolecular synthon of Gautam Desiraju and the molecular synthon that was proposed for organic synthesis by E. J. Corey.

Gautam Desiraju second area of contribution focuses on weakly activated groups like the C-H group can act as donors of hydrogen bonds in molecular and biomolecular systems. These weak hydrogen bonds had been discussed sporadically since the 1930, but it was only after the 1980s that the idea of a weakly activated group forming hydrogen bonds gained acceptance in the chemical community. Gautam Desiraju was among the few structural chemists who argued in those early days that the C-H..O and other weak interactions have a hydrogen bond character.

Gautam Desiraju has published around 479 research papers and a total of 512 publications as given in the web of science in addition to the three books on crystal engineering and hydrogen bonding, he has edited three multi-author books on these topics in structural chemistry. He has guided the Ph.D. work of nearly 40 students over the past 43 years.

His research articles are most cited with H-index and has been recognised by awards such as the Alexander von Humboldt Forschungspre is in 2000, the ISA Medal for Science in 2018 of the university of Bologna, the van der Waals Prize in 2023 of ICNI Strasbourg, and the TWAS price in Chemistry in 2000(G.R., Supramolecular Synthons in Crystal Engineering. A New Organic Synthesis, 1995).

He has been President of the international union of crystallography for the triennium in year of 2011 to 2014. He has been conferred the first 'Arrive Guru' award in 2022 of Karnataka University, Dharwad. He is a member of the India Science-20 Secretariat in G20 India Presidency in the year 2023. He is the author of a book on the Constitution of India and governance structures (2022) entitled "Bharat: India 2.0" (Arunan, 1013).

- **Animesh Chakravorty :**

Animesh Chakravorty was born 30 June 1935 in Bengal, India. He is inorganic chemist. His educated (B.Sc., M.Sc.) from Calcutta University. His Ph.D. completed in 1961 under Basu's supervision. Chakravarti determined the single crystal spectra of Cu, Ni and Cr complexes in polarized visible light and interrupted the spectra in terms ligand filed theory. Animesh Chakravorty was awarded the Shanti Swarup Bhatnagar Prize for Science and Technology in chemistry through the council of Scientific and industrial Research., TWAS Prize, Honoracy Doctorate, DSc honoris causa, University of Burdwan and Indian National Science Academy Golden

Jubilee Research Professorship. His offered postdoctoral fellowships through Geoffrey Wilkinson at Imperial College London and by Wilkinson's student F. Albert Cotton at MIT. His joined Cotton's research group in late in 1961, in which he researched solution stability constants and structures of 3-D metal complexes of imidazole derivatives (Mukherjee, 25, Sep, 2014).

Next year, upon the suggestion of Cotton, he moved to Harvard for a second postdoctoral with Cotton's student Richard H. Holm. He joined the faculty of the Indian institute of Technology, Kanpur in 1964.

Animesh Chakravorty and co-workers research group studied synthetic and stereochemical problems of new types of complexes, and were soon noted for specializing in redox phenomena and oxidation-state manipulation. Eventually appointed head of chemistry at IIT Kanpur, in 1977, he joined the Indian Association for the Cultivation of Science in Kolkata as head of inorganic chemistry. After three years, beginning with Akhil Ranjan Chakravarty, Animesh Chakravorty guided 58 doctoral students. his last doctoral student submitted his dissertation in 2006. Animesh Chakravorty has published more than 300 research articles, 20 review articles and several chapters(Chakravorty, 20 March 2015).

- <u>**Prafulla Chandra Ray**</u> :

Prafulla Chandra Ray born on 2nd August 1861 succeeded in Raruli-Katipara, Bangladesh. His lunar name was Harish Ro. Prafulla's mother Bhuvanmohini Devi was educated with liberal thoughts. The family moved to Kolkata when Prafulla was nine years old and he studied at Hare School. Later he went to Albert School. And after passing the entrance examination in 1879, he started his studies at the Metropolitan College (now Vidyasagar College). Prafulla also studied chemistry at Presidency College and it became his favourite subject; He set up a laboratory at home and started experimenting. In 1882, Prafulla won a scholarship to the University of Edinburgh, UK, and graduated there in 1885. Staying in Edinburgh to do research, he D.Sc. in 1887 and was awarded the "Hope Prize" for his thesis on "Conjugated Sulphates of the Copper-Magnesium Group: A Study of Isomorphous Mixtures and Molecular Combinations". Prafulla Chandra Ray, known as the "Father of Indian Chemistry", is a well-known Indian scientist and teacher who is one of the "modern" Indian chemical researchers.

He discovered the stable compound mercuric nitrate in 1896 and in 1901 founded Bengal Chemical and Pharmaceutical Works Limited, the first pharmaceutical company in India.

At the same time, he did not support the caste system as a very passionate and devoted social worker (Banerjee, 2011).

He has won various awards such as Companion of the <u>Order of the Indian Empire</u> (CIE) in 1912, <u>Knight Bachelor</u> in 1919, Fellow of the <u>Chemical Society</u> (FCS) in 1902, Foundation Fellow of the <u>National Institute of Sciences of India</u> (FNI) in 1935 and Fellow of the <u>Indian Association for the Cultivation of Science</u> (FIAS) in 1943 **(Proceedings of the Chemical Society, 1902).**\

References:

Chemistry Nobel Laureates (2009). Nobel Foudation.

CNR Rao is the winner of the 2011 Ernesto Illy Trieste Science Prize(2014). The Brazilian Academy of Science.

Amunts, A., & et. al. (2014). Structure of the yeast mitochondrial large ribosomal subunit. *Science*, 343 (6171):1485-1489.

Arunan, E. B. (2013). *Chemistry in India:Unlocking the Potential*. Angewandte Chemie International Edition, 52, 114.

Arvind, G. (2019). *Kamala Sohonie*. Indian National Science Academy.

Banerjee, S. (2011). Acharya Prafulla Chandra Ray: An epitome of scientific attitude and human values. *Breakthrough, 15 (1)*.

C. N.R Rao and his contributions (2011). Science & Tech journal of India.

Chakravorty, A. (2015). *Indian Scientist*. Bengali Indian academic and a professor of chemistry.

Chatterjee, A. (2019). *Sci-Illustrate*.

Common root: Tamil Nadu gets its third laureate (2009). Times of India.

Dasgupta, S. (2022). Darshan Ranganathan: 4 June 1941–4 June 2001. *Journal Article 27 , 903-919*.

Desiraju, G. R. (2011). *Crystal Engineering. A Textbook*. World Scientific.

Fernández, I. S., et. al. (2013). Molecular Architecture of a eukaryotic traslational initiation complex. *Science*, 6160.

G.R.D. (1989). Crystal Engineering. The Design of Organic Solids. *Elsevier*.

G.R.D. (1995). *Supramolecular Synthons in Crystal Engineering. A New Organic Synthesis*. Angewandte Chemie International Edition Engl. 34,2311.

Google honours Indian chemist Asima Chatterjee on 100th birthday (2017).India Times.

Gupta, S. (2002). *THE STORY OF DR. YELLAPRAGADA SUBBA ROW*. An Indian Scient in America.

How Kamala Sohonie Defied Gender Bias & Became the First Indian Woman PhD in Science. (2017). The Better India.

Kapur, S. &. (1998). Dr. Yellapragada Subbarao (1895-1948): The man and the method. *Indian Journal of Experimental Biology 36 (11).*

Khan, R. (2019). *Darshan Ranganathan: Self-Made Pioneer In Organic Chemistry* . Indian Women in History.

Koscak, M. (2019). The discovery of adenosine triphosphate and the establishment of its structure. *Journal of the History of Biology*, 145-154.

Mukherjee, R. N. (2014). Animesh Chakravorty-an era of inorganic chemistry. *Current Science, 107, 6.*

(31 Dec 2011). *No. 60009.* The London Gazette.

Pakrashi, S. C. (2012). *Asima Chatterjee.*

Proceedings of the Chemical Society. (1902). *Proceedings of the Chemical Society* (p. 18 (254) 160). Proceedings of the Chemical Society.

Rao, A. K. (2016). History. *Current Science, 111(5).*

Ritesh, K. (2017). *Kamala Sohonie - Woman, Who Established the Nutritive Value of the Plants, Consumed by Poor People.*

Tha Glass Ceiling:The why and therefore (2012). Vigyansagar Govt. of India.

The Shaping of Indian Science (2003). In *Indian Science Congress Association , Presidential Addresses by Indian Science Congress Association* (p. 1036). Published by Orient Blackswan.

Women Scientists of India: Dr. Asima Chatterjee – Google Arts & Culture. (2017).Google Cultural Institute.

CHAPTER THREE

Sir Prafulla Chandra Ray: A Revolutionary Indian Scientist

-Mr. P.B. Nagore, Dr. K. G. Mane and Dr. B. T. Vibhute

Prafulla Chandra Ray was an eminent historian, Indian chemist, philanthropist, educationist, and industrialist. He was born on 2 August 1861 and on 16 June 1944) (1.Obituary, 1944). The credit for establishing the first modern Indian research school in chemistry goes to him. He is recognized as the father of chemistry in India (2.Dasgupta, 2011).

The Royal Society of Chemistry honored his work with the first ever Chemical Landmark Plaque outside Europe. He was the founder of India's first pharmaceutical company, Bengal Chemicals & Pharmaceuticals. He authored A History of Hindu Chemistry from the Earliest Times to the Middle of the Sixteenth Century in1902.

He was admitted to the Albert School in 1876. Due to his focused self-study over the previous two years, his teachers observed he was more advanced than the rest of the students in his class. In 1878, he cleared the matriculation exams with a first division. Later, he took admission to the Metropolitan Institution, as a First Arts(FA) student, where Surendranath Banerjee, the prominent Indian nationalist and future president of the Indian National Congress (3.Majumdar, 523–533.) was his English teacher.

Primarily he focused on history and literature but chemistry was then a mandatory subject in the FA degree. He attended physics and chemistry lectures at the Presidency College as there were no facilities for sciences at his college (3.Majumdar, 523–533.). He get attracted to the chemistry courses taught by Alexander Pedler, an inspiring lecturer, and experimentalist who was among the earliest chemistry researcher in India. Momentarily fascinated by experimental science, he decided to make chemistry, a career option, as he recognized his country's future would greatly depend on his progress in science (1.Obituary, 1944). His passion for experimentation led him to set up a mini chemistry laboratory at a classmate's residence and reproduced some of Pedler's demonstrations (1.Obituary, 1944). He passed from the University of Calcutta as a student of chemistry, with a view to pursuing higher studies in the field (4. Bose, 1962).

Then, he applied for a Gilchrist Prize Scholarship while studying for his B.A. examination; which required a knowledge of at least 4 languages. He won one of the two scholarships and enrolled as a B.Sc. student at the University of Edinburgh without completing his original degree (3.Majumdar, 523–533.) then he sailed for the United Kingdom in August 1882, aged 21 (3.Majumdar, 523–533.).

At Edinburgh, he began his chemistry studies under Alexander Crum Brown and his demonstrator John Gibson, a former student of Brown's who had also studied under Robert Bunsen at the University of Heidelberg. He completed his B.Sc. in 1885 (5. Chakravorty, 2015). After this, he embarked on his doctoral studies. His thesis advisor Crum Brown was an organic chemist, but he was interested in inorganic chemistry at a time when research in the field appeared to be making limited progress compared to organic research. After rigorous review of available literature, he thought to explore the specific natures of structural affinities in double salts as the subject of his thesis. Within this area, he chose to research metal double sulfates (5. Chakravorty, 2015).

Numerous double sulfates occurred in nature as mineral salts were reported. The double sulfates are result of natural combination of sulfates of bivalent metals with monovalent metal sulfates in a 1:1 ratio, chemically distinct from their original constituent species. By the 1850, many sulfates had been synthesized artificially, including ammonium iron (II) sulfate called "Mohr's salt" by Karl Friedrich Mohr. Prior to Ray's taking up the problem, in 1886, Percival Spencer Umfreville Pickering and Emily Aston had concluded in their paper that double-double and higher-order sulfate salts did not exist as definite structures, deeming Vohl's experimental findings inexplicable (5. Chakravorty, 2015). While Ray noted such findings placed Vohl's research in doubt, he reasoned "the position was unclear and further research was called for." (5. Chakravorty, 2015)

Ray was awarded the Hope Prize which allowed him to work on his research for a further period of one year after completion of his doctorate. His thesis title was "Conjugated Sulphates of the Copper-magnesium Group:

A Study of Isomorphous Mixtures and Molecular Combinations". (6.Petitjean, Jami, & Moulin, 1992).

Scientific research

Around 1895 Prafulla Chandra started his work in the field of discovering nitrite chemistry which turned out to be extremely effective. In 1896, he published a paper on preparation of a new stable chemical compound: mercurous nitrite (6.Petitjean, Jami, & Moulin, 1992). This work made way for a large number of investigative papers on nitrites and hyponitrites of different metals, and on nitrites of ammonia and organic amines (7. Petitjean, Jami, & Moulin, 1992). He and his students had crumbled this field for several years, leading to a long discipline of research laboratories. Prafulla Chandra said that it was a new chapter in life that started with the unanticipated discovery of mercurous nitrite (7. Petitjean, Jami, & Moulin, 1992). Prafulla Chandra, in 1896, noticed the formation of a yellow crystalline solid with the reaction of excess mercury and dilute nitric acid (7. Samanta, Goswami, & Chakravorty, 2011). The ionic reactions involved are (7. Samanta, Goswami, & Chakravorty, 2011)

$2Hg^0 \rightarrow Hg_2^{2+} + 2e^-$ (Net reaction in presence of **excess mercury**)

$NO_3^- + 4H^+ + 3e^- \rightarrow NO(\uparrow) + 2H_2O$

$NO_3^- + 2H^+ + 2e^- \rightarrow NO_2^- + H_2O$

$Hg_2^{2+} + 2NO_2^- \rightarrow Hg_2(NO_2)_2 (\downarrow)(\text{yellow crystals})$

This result was first published in the Journal of the Asiatic Society of Bengal. That was forthwith noticed by Nature magazine on 28 May 1896 (7. Petitjean, Jami, & Moulin, 1992). Thermodynamically unstable mercurous nitrite survives because of its kinetic stability under the experimental condition of its preparation.

Ammonium nitrite synthesis in pure form through double displacement ammonium between chloride and silver nitrite is one of the notable contributions of P. C. Ray. He proved that the pure ammonium nitrite is indeed stable by bring to pass a lot of experiments and explained then it can be sublimed even at 60 °C without decomposition.

$NH_4Cl + AgNO_2 \rightarrow NH_4NO_2 + AgCl$

On a conference of the Chemical Society in London, he submitted the result. Nobel laureate William Ramsay congratulated him for his achievement. On 15 August 1912 Nature magazine published the news of 'ammonium nitrite in tangible form' and the determination of the vapour density of 'this very fugitive salt'. The Journal of Chemical Society, London published the experimental details in the same year (8. Chakravorty, 2014).

He prepared a lot of such compounds by double displacement. After that he worked on mercury alkyl- and mercury alkyl aryl-ammonium nitrites.

$RNH_3Cl + AgNO_2 \rightarrow RNH_3NO_2 + AgCl$

He started a new Indian School of Chemistry in 1924. Ray was president of the 1920 session of the Indian Science Congress (7. Petitjean, Jami, & Moulin, 1992).

He was a synthetic Inorganic chemist with active research in organic molecules and reactions more specifically to thio-organics. The initial work that made him famous was based on the chemistry of inorganic and organic nitrites, he was regarded as *"Master of Nitrites"*. (7. Petitjean, Jami, & Moulin, 1992).'

Prafulla Chandra retired from the Presidency College in 1916, and joined the Calcutta University College of Science as its first "*Palit Professor of Chemistry*", a chair named after Taraknath Palit. Here also he got a dedicated team and he started working on compounds of gold, platinum, iridium etc. with mercaptyl radicals and organic sulphides. A number of papers were published on this work in the Journal of the Indian Chemical Society.

He retired from active service in 1936, at the age of 75, and became professor emeritus. He had written 107 papers in all branches of Chemistry by 1920 (6.Petitjean, Jami, & Moulin, 1992).

In 1922, he donated money to establish Nagarjuna Prize to be awarded for the best work in chemistry (6.Petitjean, Jami, & Moulin, 1992). In 1937, another award, named after Ashutosh Mukherjee, to be awarded for the best work in zoology or botany, was established from his donation. (7. Petitjean, Jami, & Moulin, 1992)

Academic honours and fellowships

He bagged the Faraday Gold Medal of the University of Edinburgh in 1887 (4. Bose, 1962) He was a fellow of the Royal Asiatic Society of Bengal (FRASB) (10. Singh, 2021). He was the foundation fellow of the National Institute of Sciences of India (FNI; 1935) (10. Singh, 2021) and of the Indian Association for the Cultivation of Science (FIAS; 1943) (10. Singh, 2021) (11.Harsha & Nagaraja, 2010).

Bibliography

1.Obituary: Sir Prafulla Chandra Ray (1944). *Journal of the Indian Chemical Society*., 253-160.

2.Dasgupta, U. (2011). *Science and Modern India: An Institutional History,* C. ISBN 978-81-317-2818-5.: Pearson Education India.

3.Majumdar, S. K. (2011). Acharya Prafulla Chandra Ray: A Scientist, Teacher, Author and a Patriotic Entrepreneur" (PDF). Indian Journal of History of Science. *2011*, 523-533.

4. Bose, D. M. (1962). Acharya Prafullachandra Ray: A Study. *Science and Culture.*, 28 (11): 493-500.

5. Chakravorty, A. (2015). The Doctoral Research of Acharya Prafulla Chandra Ray. *Indian Journal of History of Science.* , 50 (3), 429-437.

6.Petitjean, P., Jami, C., & Moulin, A. M. (1992). *Science and Empires: Historical Studies about Scientific Development and European Expansion.* pp. 66–. ISBN 978-0-7923-1518-6.: Springer.

7. Petitjean, P., Jami, C., & Moulin, A. M. (1992). *Science and Empires: Historical Studies about Scientific Development and European Expansion.* pp. 66–. ISBN 978-0-7923-1518-6.: Springer.7. Samanta, S., Goswami, S., & Chakravorty, A. (2011). On mercurous nitrite and a basic mercurous nitrate derivative. *Indian Journal of Chemistry.* , 50 A,(2), 137-140.

8. Chakravorty, A. (2014). The Chemical Researches of Acharya Prafulla Chandra Ray,. *Indian Journal of History of Science..*, 49 (4): 361–370.

9. Das, A. K. (2020). Thermodynamic and Kinetic Aspects of the Stability of Sir P. C. Ray's Mercurous Nitrite Compound. *Resonance.*, 25: 787–799.

10. Singh, R. (2021). Revolutionary in the Garb of a Scientist". Science India. . *Science India*, 19 (5): 48.

11.Harsha, N. M., & Nagaraja, T. N. (2010). The History of Hindu Chemistry' A Critical Review. *Ancient Science of Life.*, 30 (2): 58–61.

CHAPTER FOUR

Contribution of Indian Scientists to Recent Advancement in Fluorescence Applications

-Dr. K. G. Mane and Mr. P. B. Nagore

What is Fluorescence?

The word fluorescence comes from fluorspar, one of many substances which emit light while they are being radiated but whose light disappears when the radiation is cut off, whereas phosphorescent materials continuously emit light even after some time.

It is the one form of luminescence. Many times, the emitted light possesses a higher wavelength and acquires lower photon energy than absorbed light radiation. An appreciable example of fluorescence is noticeable when the radiation absorbs in the UV region (not visible to the naked eye) and emits light in the visible range of the EM spectrum. This phenomenon gives a distinct color to the fluorescent substance which can be seen only when the substance gets exposed to UV radiation (1. K.G. Mane, 2018).

Fluorescence has numerous practical applications, such as chemical sensors (fluorescence spectroscopy), mineralogy, gemology, medicine, biological detectors, labeling, dyes, cosmic-ray detection, cathode-ray tubes, and vacuum fluorescent displays. Its most common routine application is in LED lamps,fluorescent lamps, and gas-discharge, in which a fluorescent-coated layer converts UV or blue light into the form of longer-wavelength light, which results in white light (2. Nan Ouyan, 2022).

Fluorescence also occurs often in nature in certain minerals and several biological forms in all the domains of life. It may be stated as *bio fluorescence*, specifying that the term fluorophore is nothing but a part of a living organism as well as of organic and inorganic materials. Since, the fluorescence is owed to a definite chemical, which can also be fabricated artificially in most cases. Such a substance is named *fluorescent* material.

Nowadays fluorescence has emerged as a powerful modern technology in chemical and biological research in the vision of its usefulness in several applications. Tools that are developed by using fluorescence spectroscopy, come into our lives in various forms. Many gadgets used in routine tests for diagnostic purposes in clinics, devices, etc., are based on fluorescence. Even for monitoring the pollution in metropolises, and even genomes sequencing is also based on fluorescence. There are very few areas in modern research in chemistry as well as biology where this fluorescence-based measurement is not used. So, Fluorescence has gained more importance in modern research areas for several reasons. Here we present, a contribution of some Indian scientists to this important phenomenon (3. Amitabha Cha ttopadhyay, 2016).

Amitabha Chattopadhyay

He is a distinguished Indian scientist working in different areas of biophysics, membrane, and receptor biology.Presently, he is a CBF at the Center for Cellular and Molecular Biology. He has worked as the founding dean of AcSIR. Besides, he is an eminent visiting professor at the IIT, Bombay, adjunct professor at the Jawaharlal Nehru University (New Delhi), Tata Institute of Fundamental Research, Indian Institute of Science Education and Research (Kolkata), Swinburne University of Technology (Australia), and honorary professor at the Jawaharlal Nehru Centre for Advanced Scientific Research (Bangalore).

He was elected as a Fellow of the RSC in 2013 and RSB in 2017. He has authored more than 300 research papers with an h-index of 67.In 2016, Chattopadhyay won 'The World Academy of Sciences in Biology' for his pivotal contribution in understanding the role of membrane cholesterol in the organization and function in healthy and diseased conditions.

Education

He received B.Sc. with honors in chemistry from St. Xavier's College (Kolkata) in 1977, M.Sc. from IIT Kanpur in 1980, and Ph.D. from State University of New York (SUNY) at Stony Brook in 1987. Further, he was a postdoctoral fellow at the University of California, Davis.

Research

His work is dedicated to monitoring organization, utility and dynamics of biological membranes in diseased as well as in healthy conditions (4. Amitabha Chattopadhyay, 2016). His research group has applied technologically advanced and innovative, sensitive and novel techniques which is based on very much useful fluorescence spectroscopy for observing membrane-mimetic media as well as monitoring solvent relaxation in membranes and proteins. (5. Roopali Saxenaa, 2014). His group focuses on the role of membrane cholesterol in regulating the organization, dynamics and function of G protein-coupled receptors (GPCRs) (6. Amitabha Chattopadhyay, 2018), Pioneering work from his group showed that membrane cholesterol is necessary for the function and organization of GPCRs (7. Amitabha Chattopadhyay1 · Samares C. Biswas1 · Raju Rukmini1 · Satyen Saha2, 2021).

In addition, his work has provided novel insight in the role of membrane cholesterol in the entry of pathogens into host cells. He has used fluorescence-based microscopic approaches such as Fluorescence Recovery After Photobleaching (FRAP), Fluorescence Correlation Spectroscopy (FCS), and Fluorescence Resonance Energy Transfer (FRET) to provide useful insight into organization, dynamics and function of membrane receptors (8. Ajuna Arora, 2004).

Thimmaiah Govindaraju

He was awarded by Swarna Jayanti Fellowship for 2015-2016 from the DST, Govt. of India in 2015, Sir C V Raman Young Scientist Award in 2014, Govt of Karnataka. 2015 CRSI Bronze Medal, Chemical Research Society of India (CRSI) for the year 2016. 2011 INSA Medal for Young Scientist (2011): Indian National Science Academy, New Delhi. 2011 Innovative Young Biotechnologist Award, DBT, Ministry of Science and Technology, Govt. of India

He is an eminent scientist in the Bioorganic Chemistry, Laboratory at Jawaharlal Nehru Centre for Advanced Scientific Research, Bengaluru.

The honours and awards conferred on T Govindaraju include Shanti Swarup Bhatnagar prize in 2021 for chemical sciences_He was a Fellow of RSC(London) in 2019, honored by CDRI Award for Excellence in Drug Research, CSIR-Central Drug Research Institute, Lucknow, India in 2017, IPS-Young Scientist Award by Indian Peptide Society in 2017 and MRSI Medal in 2017 from Materials Research Society of India.

He is a scientist in the Bioorganic Chemistry Laboratory in areas which lie at the intersection of chemistry, biology and biomaterials science, and in particular, on problems related to Alzheimer's disease, peptide chemistry, molecular probes, molecular architectonics, nanoarchitectonics and biomimetics.

He and his team has developed a new technologyplatform for fluorometric detection of pathogens such as viruses by measurement of fluorescent light emitted.

The potential of the new technology has been demonstrated for the detection of Covid-19 virus SARS-CoV-2 and also used to detect other DNA or RNA pathogens such HIV, influenza, HCV, Zika Ebola and other mutating and evolving pathogens [6].

Education

He has completed M. Sc. in 2000 from Bangalore University, Bengaluru. Received Ph.D. in 2005 from National Chemical Laboratory, Pune and Postdoctoral Research from University of Wisconsin-Madison, Madison, USA. He was a Alexander von Humboldt Foundation Research Fellow from 2006 to 2008, Max Planck Institute of Molecular Physiology, Dortmund, Germany.

Research

His research interests are at the biomaterials science, interface of chemistry, biology and focused on the theme of chemical biology of **'functional and disease amyloids'** (8. Ajuna Arora, 2004) (9. Pandeeswar Makam, 2018). With expertise in organic synthesis, peptide chemistry, bioconjugate chemistry, biophysical techniques and chemical biology (10. Y. V. Suseela, 2018) (11. Debabrata Maity, 2013), His research involved in solving challenging problems related to human health and society. Novel concepts and research themes in basic and applied interdisciplinary sciences have emerged from his laboratory (12. K Rajasekhar, 2017) (13. Yelisetty Venkata Suseela, Analysis & Sensing,).

Binoy Kumar Saikia

The Council of Scientific and Industrial Research, the apex agency of the Government of India for scientific research, awarded him the Shanti Swarup Bhatnagar Prize for Science and Technology, one of the highest Indian science awards, in 2021, for his contributions in the field of science and technology.

He is a Principal Scientist at North East Institute of Science and Technology, Jorhat (NEIST), Assam, India. He is also the Group Leader of the Coal and Energy Research Group in the Materials Science and Technology Division of NEIST.

Dr. Saikia is presently an associate member of the Indian Institute of Chemical Engineers, a Fellow member of the Geological Society of India (FGS), member of the Mining Geological and Metallurgical Institute of India (MGMI).

He has received Prof. (Dr.) M P Singh memorial coal science award-2019 for the outstanding contribution to coal chemistry and technology. He is also a recipient of the Dr. R.P Bhatnagar Award (2015-16) from The Mining, Geological & Metallurgical Institute of India (MGMI) for his outstanding contribution to mineral beneficiation. Holder of IIME Coal Beneficiation Award (Academic/Industry) in 2015, Award for Honourable Mention Technical Paper in International Pittsburgh Coal Conference, USA, and MESA (Mineral Engineering Science Association of India) Award-2014. In the same year he received Rajiv Gandhi Excellence Award-2012 from the Union Minister of Coal, Govt. of India.

Education

He completed B. Sc. Chemistry in 1998 from Debraj Roy College, Dibrugarh University, Dibrugarh, Assam, India, M.Sc., Inorganic Chemistry, 2001, Guwahati University, Guwahati, Assam, India and Ph.D. in Chemistry, 2008, from CSIR-North East Institute of Science & Technology, Jorhat.

Research

His research interests span energy and environment in general and in particular chemistry and technology of coal (14. Anusuya Boruah, 2020), carbon and nano-materials, atmospheric aerosols (15. Tonkeswar Das, 2019), and air pollution (US Patent No. US 2021/0292172 A1, 2021). He has developed and patented, both in India and the US, a technology for the production of blue-fluorescent carbon quantum dots from Indian coal (17. A Boruah, 2022) (US Patent No. 10655061, 2020).

Bibliography

1. K.G. Mane, P. N. (2018). Synthesis, Photophysical, Electrochemical and Thermal Investigation of Anthracene Doped 2-Naphthol Luminophors and their Thin Films for Optoelectronic Devices. *J Fluoresc* , 1023-1028.

2. Nan Ouyan, L. H. (2022). Application of fluorescent nano-biosensor for the detection of cancer bio-macromolecular markers. . *Polymer Testing*, 107746.

3. Amitabha Cha ttopadhyay. (2016, 3 5). *Deccan Chronicle Technology and Science*. Retrieved from https://www.deccanchronicle.com/science/

science/050316/fluorescence-nowpowerful-tool-in-scientific-research-expert.html

4. Amitabha Chattopadhyay, S. H. (2016). Dynamic Insight into Protein Structure Utilizing Red Edge Excitation Shift, . *Accounts of Chemical research,*, 12-16.

5. Roopali Saxenaa, 1. S. (2014). Location, dynamics and solvent relaxation of a nile redbased phase-sensitive fluorescent membrane probe,. *Chemistry of Lipids and Physics,*, 1-8.

6. Amitabha Chattopadhyay, R. C. (2018). Light induced charge and energy transport in nucleic acids and proteins: general discussion,. *Faraday Discuss*, 153-180.

7. Amitabha Chattopadhyay1 · Samares C. Biswas1 · Raju Rukmini1 · Satyen Saha2, 3. ·. (2021). Lack of Environmental Sensitivity of a Naturally Occurring Fluorescent Analog of Cholesterol. *Journal of Fluorescence, ,* 1401-1407.

8. Ajuna Arora, H. R. (2004). Influence of cholesterol and ergosterol on membrane dynamics: a fluorescence approach, . *Biophysical and Biochmical communication,*, 920-926.

9. Pandeeswar Makam, R. S. (2018). SERS and fluorescence-based ultrasensitive detection of mercury in water. *Biosensor and Bioelectronics*, 556-564.

10. Y. V. Suseela, N. N. (2018). Far-red fluorescent probes for canonical and non-canonical nucleic acid structures: current progress and future implication . *Chem. Soc. Rev*, 1098-1131.

11. Debabrata Maity, D. K. (2013). FRET-based rational strategy for ratiometric detection of Cu 2+ and live cell imaging . *Sensors and Accuators B : Chemical, ,* 831-837.

12. K Rajasekhar, C. J. (2017). A red-NIR emissive probe for the selective detection of albumin in urine samples and live cells, . *Org. Biomol. Chem.,,* 1584-1588.

13. Yelisetty Venkata Suseela, P. S. (Analysis & Sensing,). Cover Feature: Mitochondria-Specific Recognition of G-Quadruplexes by a Flavylium-Based Turn-On Near-Infrared Rotor Probe . *2021*, 131-131.

14. Anusuya Boruah, M. S. (2020). Blue-emitting fluorescent carbon quantum dots from waste biomass sources and their application in fluoride ion detection in water,. *Journal of Photochemi*, 111940.

15. Tonkeswar Das, B. K. (2019). Blue-fluorescent and biocompatible carbon dots derived from abundant low-quality coals . *Journal of*

Photochemistry and Photobiology B: Biology, 1-11.

16. B.K.Saikia et al ., F. o.-t. (2021). *US Patent No. US 2021/0292172 A1.*

17. A Boruah, B. K. (2022). Chemical fabrication of efficient blue luminescent carbon quantum dots from coal washery rejects (waste) for detection of Hg2+ and Sr2+ ions in water,. *Chemistry select,,* e202104567,.

18. B. K. Saikia, e. P.-f.-b. (2020). *US Patent No. 10655061.*

The Father of Indian Ethnobotany: Dr. S. K. Jain

-Mr. Pawar R. L.

Dr. S. K. Jain - one of the pioneers of Indian Ethnobotany - was born on 30 June, 1926 in Amroha, in Uttar Pradesh, India. These were the days when schooling in rural India is devoid of. The primary schooling of this son of an agriculturist was done by full-time tutors at home. His first formal education was class 5 in 1933 in his hometown, Seohara.

Despite political disturbances and parallel waves of freedom movements, he passed High School from Baraut, Meerut in 1941 and then graduated in 1943 and earned M.Sc. degree from Allahabad University in 1946. In 1947, the year India gained independence, he started his career at Meerut College as an lecturer teaching botany classes to graduate and master students.

After a brief teaching period, Dr. Jain opted to work with various organizations engaged in botanical research. From1949-51, he was Stipendiary Trainee in Plant Taxonomy at the Indian Botanic Gardens in Calcutta and later at the Forest Research Institute in Dehradun. In 1951, he moved to New Delhi and worked on the editorial staff of the Publications Division, CSIR (1951-53). From 1953-1956 Dr. Jain had the opportunity to engage in fieldwork in the forests of India as a Senior Scientific Assistant with National Botanical Research Institute, based in Lucknow.

His nascent botanical career was groomed mainly with the Botanical Survey of India (BSI), working as a Systematic Botanist at Pune (1956-60) and then as an Economic Botanist at Allahabad and Calcutta (1960-71). He published extensively on vegetation and floristics during this period. Even at this early time in his career he had a dream to do things differently. In 1965, he earned his Ph.D. from the University of Pune for his commendable work on '*Studies on the vegetation of arid, semi-arid and some adjacent regions of western India'* under the guidance of Dr. H. Santapau, then Director of BSI. Jain continued with BSI as Deputy Director at Calcutta and Shillong (1971-77), Joint Director (1977), and then served as a Director at Calcutta until his retirement (1978-84). His research work was mainly concentrated on grasses, orchids, floristic studies, endangered species, medicinal plants, ethnobotany and economic botany.

His long-standing association with BSI and as Botanical Adviser to the Government of India influenced the expansion of technical programs and Regional Stations at BSI and also the publication of the new *Flora of India*. The influence and impact of his work is evident in government policies, on research in taxonomy, in monographic studies, explorations, and the network of botanic gardens, protected areas, and conservation of wild life. His influence is also seen in modified syllabi in universities and all-India competitive examinations, international trade in plant products, policies related to botanizing in India by foreigners, all-India training programs in taxonomy and ethnobotany, broad based publication of regional floras, work on endangered species, and role of indigenous knowledge (IK) in sustainable development.

He has been Chief Editor of *Flora of India* series (1978-84) and *Ethnobotany* (an international journal of the Society of Ethnobotanists), and a member of several distinguished committees. After retirement from BSI in 1984, Dr. Jain joined the National Botanical Research Institute, CSIR, Lucknow with the Pitambar Pant National Environment Fellowship (1984-86). In 1986, he was awarded 'Emeritus Scientist' of the Council of Scientific and Industrial Research for his project on Comparative and Deductive Studies in Ethnobotany. This work resulted in his famous book *'Dictionary of Indian Folk Medicine and Ethnobotany'*, which was presented as evidence in US courts to win India the Turmeric patent.

His drive to disseminate knowledge and exchange novel ideas on how to face new challenges in ethnobotany lead him to organize several national, regional and international symposia, seminars and training courses on taxonomy, flora, threatened plants and ethnobotany in India and many other countries. Of note, in 1994 he organized the 4[th]ISE International Congress of Ethnobiology at NBRI, Lucknow. This was one of the most successful Congresses and was well attended by over 300 delegates including 82 foreign ethnobotanists from various parts of the world. This Congress was perhaps one of the milestones in Indian ethnobotany as it brought many botanists closer to Ethnobotany and the subject found due recognition and acceptability among the masses as a core scientific discipline.

Until 50 years ago, folk medicines in India survived in two main forms – (a) as grandma's recipe in towns and (b) as unrecorded Traditional Knowledge among the village medicine men. The only records covered some household remedies practiced occasionally, but were rarely taken seriously by the scientific community. The efforts of Dr. Jain have brought about a sea-change in this direction over the last five decades. He has motivated and guided scientists from varied backgrounds (botanists, foresters, Ayurveda and Unani doctors, anthropologists, sociologists, linguists, etc.) to do intensive field work and document the traditional knowledge in an organized manner.

Now, ethnobotany is an important focus area of research for major funding agencies in India. The discipline has been instrumental to understand the scientific basis of our cultural heritage and has acted as a bridge between many social and physical sciences, and between classical botany and medical sciences. Many Research and Development organizations consider ethnomedicines as a database for plant-based drug discovery programs and herbal drug development.

Until the 1960s, journals in India were unwilling to publish works on traditional knowledge. Now we have several journals that publish 75 – 100 papers on ethnobotany every year. The efforts of Dr. Jain led universities to include Ethnobotany in graduate, post-graduate, M.Phil. and Ph.D. programs and Ethnobotany has now even been recognized as a D.Sc. degree. The subject has advanced in India so quickly that Dr. Jain himself was astonished and it compelled him to write about 'Divine Botany' and 'Dynamism in Ethnobotany'.

On August 14, 1995 (the eve of Independence Day of India), he laid the foundation for the 'Institute of Ethnobiology', which started functioning initially in NBRI, Lucknow. He is the founder of four other scientific societies, viz. International Society of Tropical Ecology, International Commission on Ethnobotany, Society of Ethnobotanists (1980) and Association for Plant Taxonomy (1998). Better known as the **'Father of Indian Ethnobotany'**, the ethnobotanical research led by Jain has made a world-wide impact and many authors in Europe and America have written in no ambiguous terms about India's leadership in this subject.

Jain has explored in all parts of India, including Andaman and Nicobar Islands, and consulted all major herbaria in India, USSR, UK, USA,

Singapore, Thailand, France, Indonesia, China, and Australia. He did not restrict himself to Indian boundaries and extended his studies to Latin America and Africa to study the active principles of medicinal plants common to these continents and India. He has described 24 new taxa. His research students and colleagues named 20 plant taxa in his honor. He has guided 12 Ph.D. students on floristics, orchids, endemism, revisionary work and ethnobotanical studies. One of the students, Dr. Prabhat Kumar Hajra, became Director of BSI.(Coyle et al., 2010)

Dr. Jain has received many prestigious Awards and Fellowships, both inside and beyond India. Most notably, he is the first Asian to receive the Distinguished Economic Botanist Award by the Society for Economic Botany (U.S.A.) in 1999 for 'Meritorious contributions to study of useful plants'. He has published 43 books and over 325 research papers on taxonomy, ethnobotany, economic botany, conservation and medicinal plants. on April 20, 2021, at age 94 Dr. Jain died peacefully at home due to COVID-19, an 'Institution', is a 'busy young researcher, highly engrossed in his studies and innovations at the age of 85'.

References:

Duarte, N. (2016, June 18). *A biography of dr. Sudhanshu Kumar Jain.* International Society of Ethnobiology. Retrieved February 20, 2023, from https://www.ethnobiology.net/biography-dr-sudhanshu-kumar-jain/

Sikarwar, R.L.S. (2017). Dr. Sudhanshu Kumar Jain (A personality) [Hindi]. *Vigyan Pragati*, 48-49.

Saklani, A.K.(2011). A bibliography of Dr. Sudhanshu K. Jain. *ISE Newsletter*, 3.

Jain V. (2018) A bibliographic overview of Dr. S.K. Jain's research work on ethnobotany. *Ethnobotany*, 29, 99-109.

Jayaraman, K. S. (1997). US patent office withdraws patent on Indian herb. *Nature*, 389 (6646), 6. https://doi.org/10.1038/37835

Jain Vartika. Two lifetime achievement awards to Dr. S.K. Jain. *Ethnobotany*. 2018;30:1.

Srinivas Ramanujan

-Dr. Sayyed S. R.

Srinivasa Ramanujan was a great Indian mathematician. He is counted among the greatest mathematicians of modern times. He was the second Indian to become a member of the Royal Society and the first to become a member of Trinity College in Cambridge. He died at a very young age, but he left behind many great achievements. Based on his talent and passion, he made wonderful inventions in mathematics and simultaneously illuminated the name of India in the whole world.

About Srinivas Ramanujan

Ramanujan was born on December 22, 1887, in the village of Kumbakonam, about 160 km nearer Madras Tamil Nadu, to a Brahmin family. His father worked as a sari store clerk in a cloth merchant's shop, while his mother was a homemaker who sang at a neighbouring temple. In December 1889 he contracted smallpox. Ramanujan's intellectual growth as a youngster differed from that of other children. Ramanujan did not learn to talk until he was three years old. As a result, his parents wondered if he was mentally ill.

However, as soon as he was enrolled in the school, everyone was astounded by his brilliance. He topped the entire district in the primary exams at the age of 10 and went to Town High School for additional education in 1898. He succeeded in all subjects, especially mathematics. After that, he enrolled in Town High School and spent six years there. In 1900 he began to work on his own in mathematics summing geometric and arithmetic series.

In nature, he was peaceful, kind, and emotional. He would take a close look at everything and begin to consider it. Ramanujan was an insatiable questioner. His professors found his queries to be a little odd at times. For example, he used to ask questions like: who was the first guy in the world?

or How far is the earth from the clouds?

His talent began to influence other students and professors at school. During his school years, he not only studied college-level mathematics but also guided college students in trigonometry. He received a Subramaniam scholarship for good grades in math and English after passing the high school examination, and he was also recognized for further college education. The principal of his school had even found that the school's examinations were meaningless to Ramanujan.

Education of Shrinivas Ramanujan

Ramanujan was shown how to solve cubic equations in 1902 and he went on to find his own method to solve the quartic. The following year, not knowing that the quintic could not be solved by radicals, he tried (and of course failed) to solve the quintic. It was in the Town High School that Ramanujan came across a mathematics book by G. S. Carr called Synopsis of elementary results in pure mathematics. This book, with its very concise style, allowed Ramanujan to teach himself mathematics. The book contained theorems, formulae and short proofs. It also contained an index to papers on pure mathematics which had been published in the European Journals of Learned Societies during the first half of the 19th century. The book, published in 1886, was of course well out of date by the time Ramanujan used it. By 1904 Ramanujan had begun to undertake deep research. He investigated some series and calculated Euler's constant to 15 decimal places. He began to study the Bernoulli numbers, although this was entirely his own independent discovery.

Ramanujan, on the strength of his good school work, received a scholarship to the Government College in Kumbakonam which he entered in the year 1904. However, the following year his scholarship was not renewed because Ramanujan devoted more and more of his time to mathematics and ignored other disciplines. Consequently, he received a perfect score in mathematics, but he failed all of his other subjects and lost his scholarship Without money he was soon in difficulties and, without telling his parents, he ran away from home at seventeen to the town of Vizagapatnam about 650 km north of Madras. He continued his mathematical work, however, and at this time he worked on hypergeometric series and investigated relations between integrals and series. He was to discover later that he had been studying elliptic functions.

In 1906 he enrolled in Pachayappa College at Madras in the First Year of Arts (FA). Even Ramanujan's teachers were stumped by some of the queries they couldn't answer. His mathematics teacher was shocked when he saw his notepad. He began to spend more time teaching Ramanujan to solve math problems. Ramanujan's teacher would solve the problem in 12 stages, but he would do it in three. Another professor, seeing his potential, encouraged him to work on the journal's difficulties in Math. Everyone recognized Ramanujan as mathematics genius. His aim was to pass the First Arts examination which would allow him to be admitted to the University of Madras. He attended lectures at Pachaiyappa's College but became ill after three months study. He took the First Arts examination and passed in mathematics but failed all his other subjects and therefore failed the examination. This meant that he could not enter the University of Madras. In the following years he worked on mathematics developing his own ideas without any help and without any real idea of the then current research topics other than that provided by Carr's book.

The end of formal education and a period of struggle

Ramanujan had a terrible time for five years after graduating from high school. At this period, India was enslaved in the United Kingdom. There was terrible poverty everywhere. Shrinivas Ramanujan had neither employment nor a degree at that time. He was constantly encouraged to follow the road of duty by his religion and respect. He was only having a deep belief in God and a strong belief in mathematics.

Namagiri Devi was considered a domestic goddess by Shrinivas Ramanujan and his family. They were angry that they could not maintain their family even if they wanted to. The unwavering faith in the goddess did not let him down despite the adversity, and he continued to study math and also worked as a math's teacher. In this job, he was earning five rupees per month and lived off that.

Shrinivas Ramanujan's contribution to mathematics

He first arrived in Madras in search of work. He went from house to house, seeking assistance from his friends. His notebooks, in which he wrote many arithmetic questions and theorems, were the main evidence of his ability. Many people, however, turned him down because he lacked a degree.

Only a few persons were aware of his abilities. Shri V. Ramaswamy Iyer, the Deputy Collector, was one of them. Mr. Iyer saw Ramanujan's potential. Although Mr. Iyer did not provide him with a job, he did arrange a monthly scholarship of Rs.25 for him through the District Magistrate Shri Ramachandra Rao so that Ramanujan may write for the Mathematical

Society's magazine.

For a year, Ramanujan contributed research articles and inquiries to the publication. Slowly but surely, everyone's gaze was drawn to him. Officer-in-Charge Sir Francis Spring and Narayan Iyer sent him to the Madras Port of Trust as an Accounting Clerk. He used to receive 30 rupees in this job.

Srinivas Ramanujan's Marriage

One day Ramanujan's mother had gone out with many of her friends. She met Janki, a 9-year-old girl. The girl's innocent look and mischievous eyes attracted Ramanujan's mother. Seeing her son's future deteriorating with mathematics, his mother married him in 1908 to a girl named Janaki. After marriage, forgetting everything and drowning in mathematics was impossible for him. As a result, Ramanujan set out in search of an excellent opportunity.

Srinivasa Ramanujan's discovery

- Ramanujan wrote more than 3000 theorems.
- Approximations to Pi and modular equations
- For five years in England, Ramanujan worked mostly in the subject of number theory.

Srinivasa Ramanujan number

- Ramanujan number is a natural number that can be represented in two different ways by the sum of the cubes of two numbers. Example, $9^3+10^3=1^3+12^3=1729$
- Ramanujan numbers are 1729, 4104, 20683, 39312, 40033 etc.

Death of Srinivasa Ramanujan

At 32, Ramanujan died at Kumbakonam, India, on April 26, 1920. The cause of his death was Hepatic amoebiasis, an intestine ailment.

References:

1. Berndt, Bruce C. (1985). *Ramanujan's Notebooks: Part I*. New York: Springer. ISBN 978-0-387-96110-
2. Berndt, Bruce C. (1999). *Ramanujan's Notebooks: Part II*. New York: Springer. ISBN 978-0-387-96794-3.
3. Berndt, Bruce C. (2004). *Ramanujan's Notebooks: Part III*. New York: Springer. ISBN 978-0-387-97503-0.

4. Berndt, Bruce C. (1993). *Ramanujan's Notebooks: Part IV*. New York: Springer. ISBN 978-0-387-94109-7.

5. Berndt, Bruce C. (2005). *Ramanujan's Notebooks: Part V*. New York: Springer. ISBN 978-0-387-94941-3.

6. Hardy, G. H. (March 1937). "The Indian Mathematician Ramanujan". *The American Mathematical Monthly*. 44 (3): 137–155. doi:10.2307/2301659. JSTOR 2301659.

7. Henderson, Harry (1995). *Modern Mathematicians*. New York: Facts on File Inc. ISBN 978-0-8160-3235-8.

8. Kanigel, Robert (1991). *The Man Who Knew Infinity: a Life of the Genius Ramanujan*. New York: Charles Scribner's Sons. ISBN 978-0-684-19259-